KU-536-923

AFRICAN CULTURE

By

Holly Duhig

WORLD CULTURES

©2017
Book Life
King's Lynn
Norfolk PE30 4LS

ISBN: 978-1-78637-196-6

All rights reserved
Printed in Malaysia

Written by:
Holly Duhig

Edited by:
Charlie Ogden

Designed by:
Evie Wright

A catalogue record for this book
is available from the British Library

PHOTO CREDITS

**Abbreviations: l-left, r-right, b-bottom,
t-top, c-centre, m-middle.**

Front cover – LuckyImages. 2 – aphotostory. 3 - Nanette Grebe. 4 – Valeriya Anufriye-
va. 5tl – Bernd Juergens. 5tm – Merydolla. 5tr – akturer. 5cl – michaeljung. 5d – sun
singer. 5cr – Gabrel. 5bl – DiversityStudio. 5bm – Sylvie Bouchard. 5br – EcoPrint.
6l – Ganibal. 6b – Puwadol Jaturawutthichai. 7l – Lenar Musin. 7r – Sergey Uryad-
nikov. 8 – Maxger. 9l – Vladimir Zhoga. 9r – Gil.K. 10 – Alessia Pierdomenico. 11 – Nort.
12 – Hosan Shaheed. 13 – atm2003. 14 – FabrikaSimf. 15 – Bluerain. 16 – Zurijeta 17 –
Lorimer Images. 18 – Alena Ozerova. 19 – Oleg Znamenskiy. 20 – Quick Shot. 21 – ariya
olasunkanmi. 22 – Ran Zisovitch. 23 – Fanfo

Images are courtesy of Shutterstock.com.
With thanks to Getty Images, Thinkstock Photo and iStockphoto.

CONTENTS

Words that look like this can be found in the glossary on page 24.

WHAT IS CULTURE?

A culture is the beliefs and ideas of a group of people. For many people, culture is very important.

Many things go into making a culture.

Food

History

Traditions

Religion

Location

Communities

WHAT MAKES A CULTURE?

Clothes

Family

Art

5

WHERE IS AFRICA?

Europe

Africa

South America

N W E S

Africa is the second largest **continent** in the world. It is south of Europe and east of South America.

Africa is home to 54 countries and over 1.2 billion people. Africa has many **unique** landscapes ranging from the dry Sahara Desert to the rainy jungles of Congo.

Sahara Desert

Jungles of Congo

COUNTRIES IN AFRICA

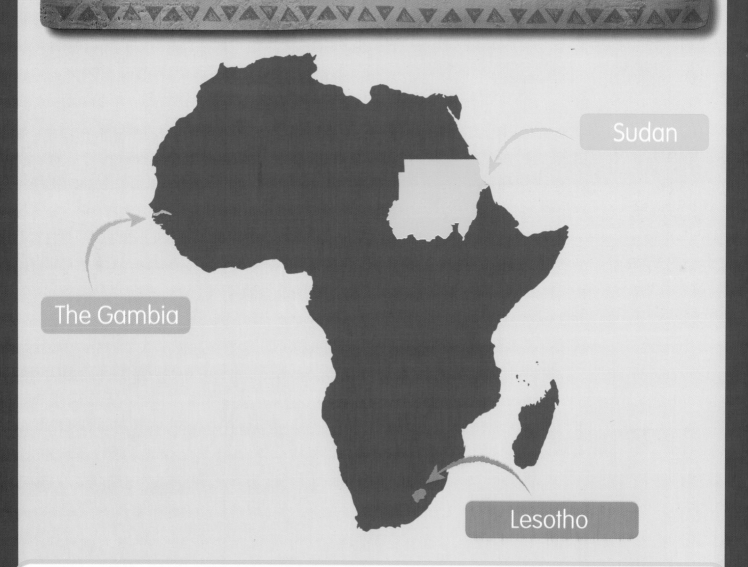

Sudan

The Gambia

Lesotho

Some countries in Africa are very big. Sudan is one of the largest countries in Africa. Other countries in Africa are very small. The Gambia is one of the smallest African countries.

The Gambia is also one of the flattest countries in the world. Other African countries, like Lesotho, are covered in mountains.

The Gambia

Lesotho

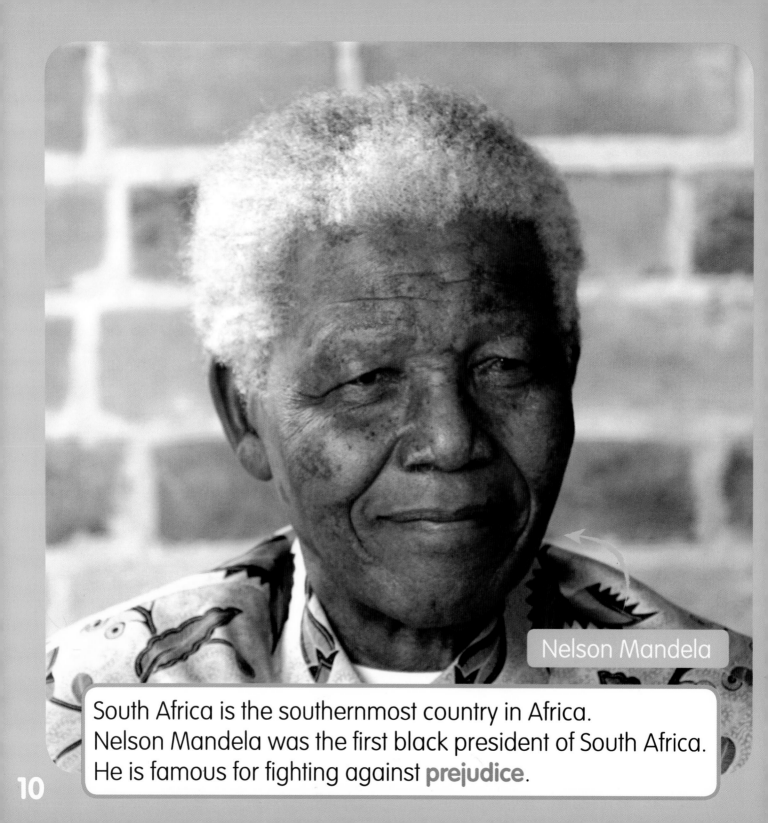

Nelson Mandela

South Africa is the southernmost country in Africa.
Nelson Mandela was the first black president of South Africa.
He is famous for fighting against **prejudice**.

Egypt is in the north of Africa. Egypt is famous for its pyramids. Pyramids are giant **tombs** built for ancient Egyptian kings, known as **pharaohs**.

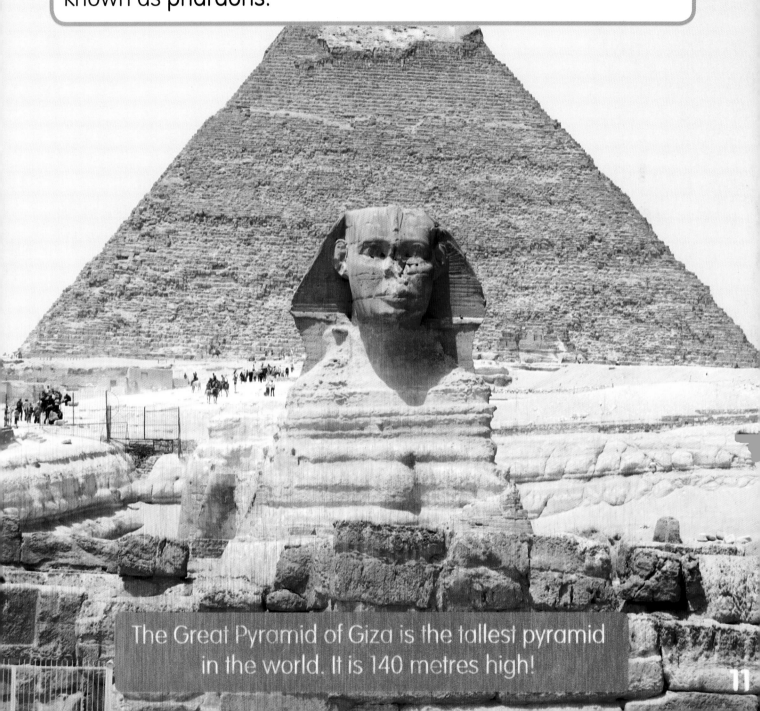

The Great Pyramid of Giza is the tallest pyramid in the world. It is 140 metres high!

MUSIC

Drums play a big part in **traditional** African music.
In Africa, drums are played to bring communities together.

Lots of African traditions involve drums, making drums an important part of African culture. In the past, for example, drums were used to **communicate** with tribes that lived miles away.

CLOTHING

Different countries in Africa have different traditional clothing. A traditional piece of clothing in Nigeria is a headscarf called a gele. These are usually brightly coloured.

In Ethiopia, women often wear dresses made of shemma. Shemma is a cloth made from white cotton. Shiny threads and colourful patterns are often added to the dresses.

RELIGION

For most people in Africa, their religion is also a part of their culture.

Many different religions are practiced in Africa. Two of the most popular religions are Christianity and Islam. People who follow Islam are called Muslims.

There are also many tribal religions unique to African culture. For example, the Igbo people worship lots of gods, each of which looks after different things in the world.

LANGUAGE

Language is very much a part of culture. Over 1,500 languages are spoken in Africa. The most widely spoken languages are Swahili, Arabic and English.

Many tribes in Africa have their own unique languages. This makes language very important to their culture because everyone who speaks their language is also part of their community.

COMMUNITIES

Dogon Women

People who are part of the same community often share the same culture. Some people in Africa, such as the Dogon people in Mali, live in small communities. The Dogon people live in villages and have their own religion.

The biggest city in Africa is Lagos. Lagos is the capital city of Nigeria. In cities like Lagos, people live in big, fast-paced communities.

Lagos, Nigeria

21

FOOD

Potjie Pot

Cooking is very important in African culture. Around 4,000 years ago, people in Africa began to make iron pots called potjies.

It is a tradition in South Africa to make a meal called potjiekos, which is cooked in these pots. Potjiekos means 'small pot food'.

GLOSSARY

communicate	to pass information between two or more people
continent	a very large area of land that is made up of many countries, like Africa and Europe
prejudice	treating people differently or unfairly for no good reason
tombs	places where the dead are buried
traditional	related to very old behaviours or beliefs
unique	the only one of its kind

INDEX